GLADIATORS

Rupert
Matthews

Gareth Stevens
PUBLISHING

Please visit our website, **www.garethstevens.com**.
For a free color catalog of all our high-quality books, call toll free 1-800-542-2595 or fax 1-877-542-2596

Library of Congress Cataloging-in-Publication Data

Matthews, Rupert.
Gladiators / by Rupert Matthews.
p. cm. — (History's fearless fighters)
Includes index.
ISBN 978-1-4824-3165-0 (pbk.)
ISBN 978-1-4824-3168-1 (6 pack)
ISBN 978-1-4824-3166-7 (library binding)
1.Gladiators — Rome — History — Juvenile literature.
2. Gladiators — History — Juvenile literature. I. Matthews, Rupert. II. Title.
GV35.M38 2016
796.8'0937—d23

First Edition

Published in 2016 by
Gareth Stevens Publishing
111 East 14th Street, Suite 349
New York, NY 10003

© Alix Wood Books

Produced for Gareth Stevens by Alix Wood Books
Designed by Alix Wood
Editor: Eloise Macgregor

Photo credits:
Cover, 1, 3, 4, 5, 17, 19, 26, 29, 35, 36, 37 bottom, 38, 39, 41, 42 © Shutterstock; 7 top, 15 © iStock; 7 bottom © BigRoloImages/Shutterstock; 8, 16, 40 © The Trustees of the British Museum; 9 © Poniol60; 11 © Ad Meskens; 12 © MatthiasKabel; 13 © Estellez/iStock; 14 © AKP/ Olschinsky; 16 top © Fotolia; 21 bottom, 30 top © DollarPhotoClub; 22 © meunierd/Shutterstock; 23 © Juan G. Aunion/Shutterstock; 24 © Carole Raddato; 25 © Curiosito; 27 © nito/Shutterstock; 28 © Fabryb13; 29 top © Álvaro Pérez Vilariño; 30 bottom © Carole Raddato; 31 © Jgaunion/Dreamstime; 32 top © Davide Ferro; 32 bottom © Matthias Kabel; 34 © Louis le Grands; 37 top © Jaap Rouwenhorst; remaining images are in the public domain

Printed in the United States of America
CPSIA compliance information: Batch #CS15GS: For further information contact Gareth Stevens, New York, New York at 1-800-542-2595.

Contents

The moment had come. All the gladiator's training was now to be put to the test. As they entered the arena they were hit by the noise of the crowd. Arenas could seat thousands of people, and the spectators were all waiting to be entertained!

The gladiators would step out onto the sandy floor. The sand was usually about 6 inches (15 cm) deep and was put there to soak up the blood. Under the sand there would often be a wooden floor with trapdoors and tunnels beneath.

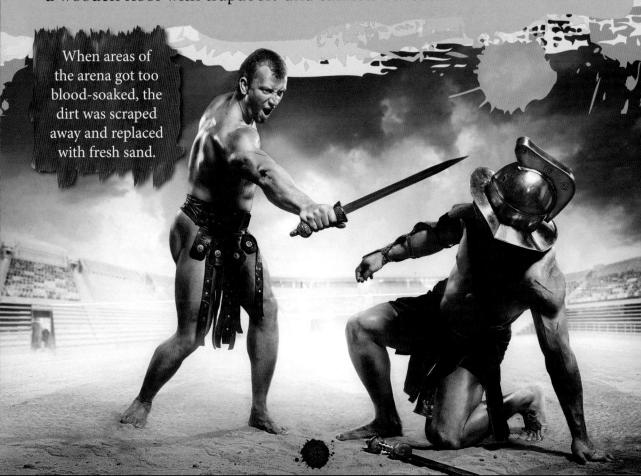

When areas of the arena got too blood-soaked, the dirt was scraped away and replaced with fresh sand.

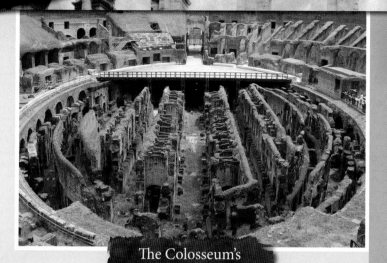
The Colosseum's
underground tunnels

The earliest gladiator contests were held in marketplaces or forums. One of the first purpose-built **amphitheaters** was built at Pompeii around 70 BCE. The first amphitheater in Rome was made of wood around 53 BCE. Two wooden semicircular theaters were moved to make one circular amphitheater, while the spectators were still seated in the two halves!

Later, the Colosseum was built in Rome. It could hold up to 50,000 spectators. It had two levels of tunnels and 32 animal pens.

The network of underground passages would be very busy during the games. Gladiators and animals were kept underground before the games began. There were trapdoors in the wooden floor. Scenery, gladiators, and even wild animals would be raised though the trapdoors into the arena above. It must have been terrifying to suddenly be faced with bright sunlight and the roaring crowd.

That's Fearless!

The audience expected gladiators to fight and die courageously. Early gladiator contests almost always ended in the death of one of the fighters. When a gladiator entered the arena, he must have known that death was quite likely.

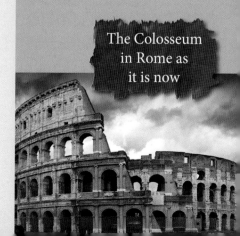
The Colosseum in Rome as it is now

Slave Gladiators

When gladiator fights first began, all gladiators were **slaves**. They had no choice about whether or not to fight, as slaves they had to do as they were told or they would be killed anyway.

It is thought that the gladiator games started in Greek areas of southern Italy. The Greeks sometimes **sacrificed** humans as part of a funeral. Around 400 BCE the sacrificial victims were allowed to fight each other to the death instead of being killed by a priest.

About one third of the population of Italy in ancient times were slaves. Most slaves worked on farms, in mines, or in workshops, only a few were house servants. Slaves could be beaten, branded, or killed by their owners for bad behavior. On the other hand, slaves could own property and work for cash in their spare time. Some slaves saved enough money to buy themselves, and so they became free.

That's Fearless!

Some slaves rose to become great men. Narcissus was an educated slave set free by his master. He got a job as secretary to Emperor Claudius and advised Claudius on who to appoint to key jobs in the Empire. When Claudius died, the new emperor, Nero, ordered Narcissus' execution. Rather than run away to save his own life, he stayed to straighten out Claudius' affairs!

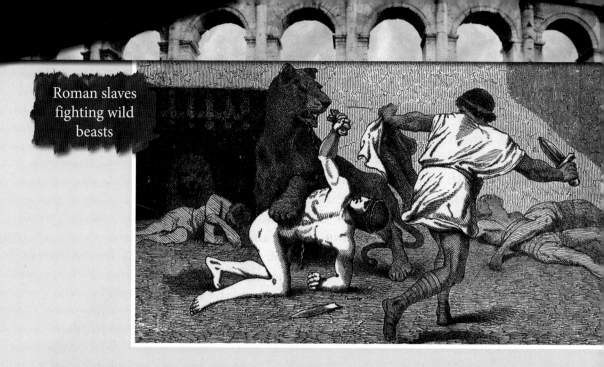

Roman slaves fighting wild beasts

Slaves were sold at auctions held in marketplaces. Each slave had to stand on a stage while a sign was held up giving his or her name, age, and where they came from, and details of their health, education, and character. If a customer was unhappy with their purchase, he or she could take the slave back for a refund within six months. Around 250,000 slaves were sold in Rome every year.

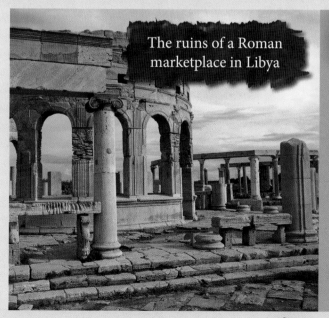

The ruins of a Roman marketplace in Libya

GLADIATOR FIGHT

The first recorded gladiator fight took place in Rome's cattle market in 264 BCE during the funeral of the nobleman Brutus Pera. Six of Pera's slaves were given weapons and split into pairs. Each pair was then told to fight to the death, the survivors were allowed to go free!

Prisoners of War

Rome fought a long series of wars against enemies across Europe. Enemy soldiers captured in battle were often sold as slaves. Because these men were experienced fighters they were often bought by gladiator trainers for use as gladiators. They could be relied upon to fight bravely and skillfully, putting on a good show for the audience.

Samnites

The first prisoners of war to be used as gladiators were **Samnites**. The Samnites were neighbors of Rome, living along the east coast of central Italy. They were famous for the superior quality of their armor, which was decorated with gold and silver. Samnite soldiers captured in a war around 200 BCE were sold in Rome as gladiators who fought to the death at funerals.

DINNER ENTERTAINMENT

In 201 BCE the Samnites were defeated by allies of Rome from **Campania**, southern Italy. At a victory feast the captured Samnite soldiers were made to fight to the death while the Campanians ate their dinner!

A Samnite gladiator helmet

Chariot racing was popular entertainment in Rome.

British Chariots

After he invaded Britain in 55 BCE, Julius Caesar sent British prisoners of war to Rome. The prisoners came complete with their chariots and trained chariot ponies. One man drove the chariot at high speed, while the second threw javelins at opponents or leaped down to use a sword on foot. The Romans called these fighters Essedarius.

Prisoners From Thrace

Rome fought a series of wars against the hill tribes of Thrace. **Thracian** gladiator prisoners fought with their own equipment, a small, rectangular shield, javelin, dagger, and a helmet with a crest.

That's Fearless!

When the supply of prisoners of war dried up, slaves were given the weapons used by Thracians or **Gauls** and trained to fight in their style.

Criminals and Volunteers

From about 100 BCE new ways of recruiting gladiators were being used. Slaves fighting to the death went out of popularity and display fights between highly skilled men became fashionable. Deaths became rarer as the value of famous gladiators rose. But the crowds still expected to see blood, so a new supply of men to kill had to be found!

People found guilty of some crimes could be sentenced to fight in the arena. Those guilty of tax evasion, **oath** breaking, or refusing to help government officials could be sentenced "ad gladitorium." They became gladiators for a specified period of time, usually up to five years. If they survived they were set free.

Serious crimes such as rebellion, murder, or treason were given the punishment of **noxii**. This meant that the person deserved to be killed in a humiliating, painful, and public way. Noxii were sent unarmed to face lions, tigers, or other wild animals. Others were given weapons to kill each other with. The really unlucky ones were forced to appear in dramatic plays that ended with their deaths.

Victims waiting to enter the arena

Venatores fighting a tiger, from a mosaic in Istanbul, Turkey

Crimes such as banditry, robbery with violence, or fire-starting could result in a man being sentenced "ad venatorium." These men were sent to fight wild animals in the arena for a set number of years. They often had less chance of survival than those sent to be gladiators.

That's Fearless!

From about 50 BCE some men volunteered to become gladiators. If a man was in debt he might become a gladiator for a number of years so that the trainer would pay off his debts. Other men are thought to have volunteered in order to escape from the authorities.

FIGHTING FOR LAUGHS

In about AD 120 a nobleman who had become poor volunteered to fight against a famous gladiator. He appeared dressed as a woman, wearing a hat decorated with ribbons and carrying a fisherman's spear! He delighted in slapping his heavily armored opponent with the spear, then skipping away. Eventually the gladiator got so tired he gave up! The audience laughed and threw money in appreciation at the man's bizarre display.

Gladiators lived or died according to how skilled they were with weapons. Training to fight with skill was an essential part of their lives. They spent hours every day practicing with their weapons so that they became able to fight in the arena.

The training camps were known as the **ludus**. Each was run by a **lanista** or manager. The ludus was usually surrounded by high walls to prevent gladiators from escaping. The gate was guarded at all times.

No real weapons were allowed inside the ludus. Gladiators were valuable and the lanista did not want them injured by accident. Also, slaves and criminals might try to use real weapons to escape. Training weapons were made of wood, with lead weights added to make them the same weight as the real weapons.

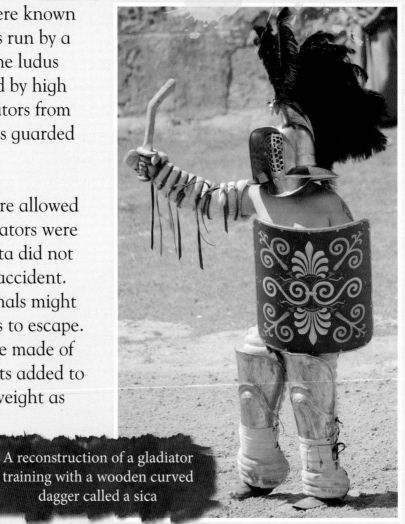

A reconstruction of a gladiator training with a wooden curved dagger called a sica

When a new man arrived in the ludus he was called a **novicius**. His training started with long runs and weightlifting to build up fitness. He then trained with different weapons and types of armor to see which suited him best. After about six months the lanista decided which weapons the man should use. He was no longer a novice, and trained for real fights.

Gladiators were expected to put on a show in the arena. They learned skills such as juggling their weapons, doing somersaults, cartwheels, leaps, and spins to put on a better display!

WOODEN ENEMY

Upright wooden posts called **palus** stood in the training ground. These were given shields, helmets, and weapons so that gladiators could practice attacking them. Gladiators were taught how to slip a blade past the shield and score a hit on the body of the opponent.

That's Fearless!

Gladiators usually trained in their underwear. Gladiators would decorate them with colored ribbons or shiny metal plates to make them look more spectacular!

Exercising in the ludus

Discipline and Routine

Gladiators never got a day off work. Every day was the same, unless it was a fight day. The routine was strict and unvarying. Gladiators spent all day every day getting ready to fight in the arena.

The day began with gladiators being woken up by servants. New gladiators slept together in large rooms without windows. They slept on sacks of straw and had rough blankets to keep warm at night. More experienced and valuable gladiators had their own rooms with comfortable beds and soft blankets. Some even had separate rooms for their wives and children.

Smaller ludus had an open space covered by sand where the gladiators trained. Larger ludus trained gladiators in an oval area the same size and shape as a fighting arena. Temporary screens were used to separate smaller areas for specialist training.

A ludus sand arena at the Roman ruins of Carnuntum, Austria

OWNER'S MARK

Each man had a tattoo on his leg that identified him as a gladiator and gave the name of his lanista. If the gladiator was sold by one lanista to another, the tattoo had to be changed.

Punishments for gladiators were harsh. Trainers had short whips to strike any gladiator who misbehaved in training. More serious punishments included being chained in a dark room for days on end, or being tied to a palus and beaten repeatedly with a long whip. As a final threat, the lanista had the right to kill any gladiator for a serious breach of discipline.

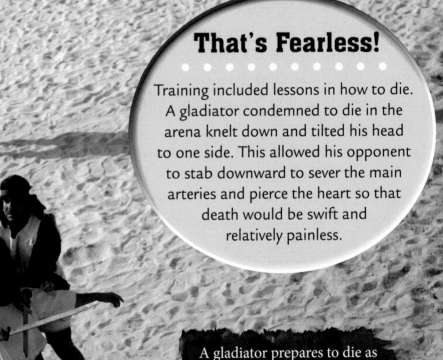

That's Fearless!

Training included lessons in how to die. A gladiator condemned to die in the arena knelt down and tilted his head to one side. This allowed his opponent to stab downward to sever the main arteries and pierce the heart so that death would be swift and relatively painless.

A gladiator prepares to die as his opponents ask whether he should be saved or not.

Food and Medical Care

Gladiators had to be kept in the peak of physical condition. Their owners wanted them to be able to fight in the arena at short notice. That meant caring for the physical well-being of the gladiators at all times.

Breakfast every day consisted of a porridge made from ground up barley and oat grains boiled in water. Lunch was made from more porridge mixed with beans and vegetables. Supper included more porridge, mixed with wood ash, which was thought to protect the body from infections. Fresh and dried fruit were always available as snacks for a hungry gladiator.

Gladiators ate a diet of porridge, porridge, and more porridge!

The evening before a fight, the gladiators were served a great banquet. Vast amounts of luxury food were served and the gladiators could eat as much as they liked. This was probably the only time that gladiators got to eat meat.

A sketch of a typical Roman banquet

THE GREAT GALEN

In AD 157 the greatest doctor in the Roman Empire, Aelius Galenus, wanted to dissect human bodies to learn more about surgery, but this was against the law. He volunteered to be the resident doctor to the gladiator ludus in the city of **Pergamon** in the hope that he could get access to dead bodies. But Galen was such a good doctor that he cured all the injured gladiators and so still had no bodies to study!

Every ludus had a team of massage workers. Their job was to ensure top quality muscle tone for the gladiators. Before and after exercise, the gladiators had a massage to loosen their muscles and to check for any minor injuries that might cause problems if left untreated.

On fight days the surgeon would stand by with tools and equipment to stitch up wounds, set broken bones, and save the lives of wounded gladiators. Among the tools a ludus surgeon used were:

scalpel to cut out fragments of weapon lodged in wounds

forceps to remove pieces of cloth or dirt from wounds

hooks to hold a wound open so it could be cleaned

saw to cut through bone to amputate a mangled limb

vinegar to clean and sterilize wounds and instruments.

Servants and Trainers

A ludus needed a large number of support staff. These jobs were often given to older or wounded gladiators who could no longer fight in the arena. A wounded gladiator was still the property of the lanista. A crippled slave was not worth much, so most lanistae kept the wounded men rather than sell them. After all, an old gladiator could pass on good advice to new ones. There were plenty of jobs on offer.

Employment Opportunities

Wanted - Cook

Gladiator food is basic, but somebody has to cook it. As our cook you will have to be able to produce high quality dishes, too, to serve the lanista's guests. Favorite snacks you will need to prepare are:

Roast dormouse This is most popular in the fall when the dormouse is very fat before hibernation

Pears poached in wine Choose from over 35 varieties of pear on sale in Rome

Serving suggestion!
Raw oyster

Snails Fry them in olive oil and garlic

Figs Dip them in honey

Oysters Don't bother cooking these, serve them raw!

Wine Mix it with water, honey, and chopped dates

Sardines Try grilling them with garlic

Cleaner Required

We need staff to make sure the rooms and courtyard are spotless at all times. We will supply a broom made from thin, supple twigs tied to a wooden pole.

Masseuse Wanted

Gladiators need regular massages to keep their muscles in good condition. Can you make the grade?

Could You Be a Door Guard?

Wanted, fierce guards to make sure no one enters or leaves the ludus without permission from the lanista. Can you handle guarding the gate day and night?

Unctores Required

Keep our gladiators' skin and muscles in good condition by rubbing them with olive oil once a day. You will need to know how to use a strigil. This curved brass tool will help you scrape off the oil and dirt from their skin.

Skilled Armorer Wanted

Making armor and weapons is a highly skilled job. Have you got the skills? We also need old gladiators to help as assistants, polishing armor, sharpening weapons, and washing fabric.

Wanted - Specialist Trainers

Are you a retired gladiator? Teach new young recruits your skills and gladiator style. Murmillos and Retiarius styles are of particular interest.

Poster Painter Needed

Join our team of poster painters. Go around the streets painting advertisements on walls. Neat handwriting and the ability to paint gladiator portraits would be desirable.

The reasons for gladiatorial combats changed over time, but originally there was only ever one reason for a fight: a funeral.

When a Roman citizen died his family were expected to hold a **munus**, a celebration of his life to which friends and neighbors would be invited. Families could show off how rich and important they were by holding huge events with food and drink, musicians, and entertainment. The earliest gladiatorial combats were held as part of a munus.

In 174 BCE the general Titus Quinctius Flaminius died. His munus lasted for three days featuring 74 gladiatorial combats! The fights were held at the festival of **Saturnalia** in December when the citizens would not be at work. This meant they would be able to attend and be impressed by his games. The event gave the Flaminius family prestige.

A statue of Romans celebrating Saturnalia, a carnival-like festival to honor the god Saturn

In 53 BCE Gaius Scribonius Curio held a munus for his father. The munus was delayed and took place just before the election for the position of Tribune, an important political post. The gladiator fights were spectacular and made Curio very popular. He then announced he was standing for election and won by many votes. Soon, all politicians were organizing gladiatorial fights just before standing for election!

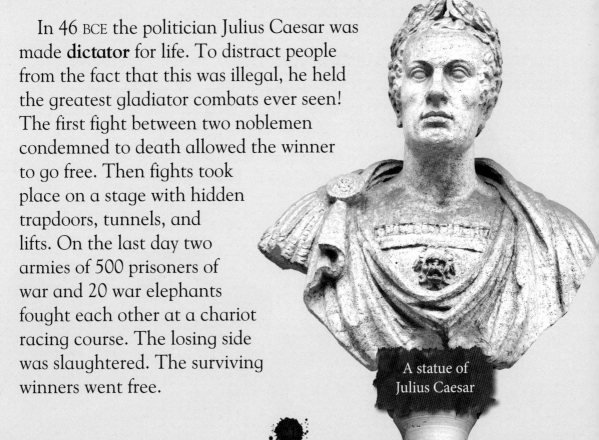

In 46 BCE the politician Julius Caesar was made **dictator** for life. To distract people from the fact that this was illegal, he held the greatest gladiator combats ever seen! The first fight between two noblemen condemned to death allowed the winner to go free. Then fights took place on a stage with hidden trapdoors, tunnels, and lifts. On the last day two armies of 500 prisoners of war and 20 war elephants fought each other at a chariot racing course. The losing side was slaughtered. The surviving winners went free.

A statue of
Julius Caesar

A Day at the Games

By about AD 50, gladiator games began to follow a pattern. Weeks before the show the man who was paying, called the **editor**, hired a lanista and his team of gladiators. They agreed on which gladiators and animals would fight, and the cost.

First to enter the arena was the editor, followed by a parade of the people and animals who would take part in the show. A priest honored the gods before the games began. Then musicians and dancers would perform. Next, wild animals such as boars, bears, or deer would be hunted by men armed with bows and spears. When all the animals were dead, clowns, acrobats, or comic actors would entertain the crowd.

After the jokes, the killing began. Men or women who had been condemned to death were dragged into the arena. They were stabbed, beheaded, or made to fight each other. Those guilty of serious crimes were thrown to lions, tigers, or wolves to be killed and eaten.

The first gladiators to enter the arena were usually on horseback. These men put on a fast-moving display, including trick riding as well as fighting with lances and swords.

The gladiatorial fights were nearly always one gladiator fighting another. This allowed the crowd to concentrate on each pair of fighters and appreciate their skills. It also meant that the games lasted a long time. Every fight was supervised by a referee who made sure that the gladiators obeyed the rules. We do not know what the rules were as no copy of them has survived. The referee could stop a fight and disqualify a gladiator for cheating.

MERCY

Each pair of gladiators fought until one gave up or they ran out of time. The editor then decided if a defeated gladiator lived or died. In most fights he was allowed to live, called "granting the **missus**." The winner was given a palm leaf and a cash prize. If time ran out the fight was declared a draw.

A referee watches during this reconstruction of a gladiator fight.

A victorious gladiator was given a cash prize at the end of his fight. The more famous a gladiator became, the more money he could expect to win.

As a gladiator became more famous he built up a following of fans who cheered him on in fights and tried to make sure he was not condemned to death if he lost. A few gladiators retired as rich men to live in comfort for the rest of their lives. The names of a few gladiators have been discovered by historians.

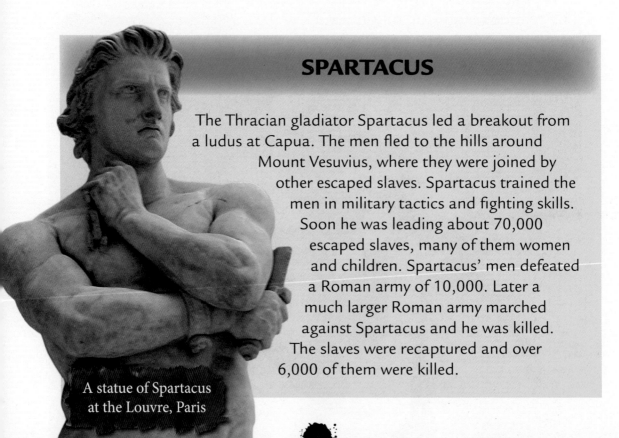

SPARTACUS

The Thracian gladiator Spartacus led a breakout from a ludus at Capua. The men fled to the hills around Mount Vesuvius, where they were joined by other escaped slaves. Spartacus trained the men in military tactics and fighting skills. Soon he was leading about 70,000 escaped slaves, many of them women and children. Spartacus' men defeated a Roman army of 10,000. Later a much larger Roman army marched against Spartacus and he was killed. The slaves were recaptured and over 6,000 of them were killed.

A statue of Spartacus at the Louvre, Paris

TETRAITES

Tetraites was a **murmillo** superstar. We know that he fought one bout in Pompeii when he defeated a man named Prudes. Cups, plates, and other pottery were made showing Tetraites in action and sold to fans wherever he appeared. The souvenirs have been found in France and Britain as well as in Italy, so Tetraites must have traveled a great deal in his career.

A murmillo

That's Fearless!

Carpophorus was a **venatores**, a fighter who fought animals. His most famous feat was to take on a rhinoceros armed with nothing but a single spear. Carpophorus was also famed for being able to defeat leopards and lions. He once fought a bear, a lion, and a leopard at the same time!

PRISCUS AND VERUS

The most famous gladiators in Rome in AD 80 were Priscus the Celt and Verus the Roman. Emperor Titus hired them to be the first gladiators to fight in the newly completed Colosseum. Their fight went on much longer than usual. When both men were exhausted, Titus stopped the fight and set both men free!

Gladiator armor was unusual, because the body was almost always left bare. The head and neck were protected by strong metal helmets. Arms and legs were covered by armor made of metal or padded cloth. Audiences wanted to see long, skillful fights. Injuries to the head, hands, arms, or legs might end the fight too quickly. Hits to the body were rare as it required great skill to hit that area and not get hurt yourself.

The armor used by gladiators was stronger and heavier than soldiers' armor. Gladiators wore armor for around 20 minutes, so they did not get as tired as soldiers who might wear armor for hours each day.

Later gladiatorial helmets had visors. These protected the face and neck, and made the gladiator unrecognizable. This helped when a gladiator had to fight a colleague from his own barracks. Even the most hardened gladiator might have found it difficult to kill a friend.

Show business demands that costumes be loud, colorful, and bright, and gladiator armor was no exception! Helmets, shields, and armor were plated with silver or gold and brightly polished. Helmets were often decorated with showy plumes and crests that would not have been used by real soldiers. Ostrich feathers were popular, so were peacock feathers, and tail feathers from pheasants. Cloth costumes were also dyed in bright colors.

WOMEN GLADIATORS

Women generally only fought other women. Women gladiators appear to have fought in murmillo armor, but without the helmet. Presumably they were left bareheaded so that the crowd could see that they were women. The chest was covered by fabric, though it is not clear if this was a simple tunic or padded armor. Female gladiators never appeared in large numbers and in AD 200 the Emperor Septimius Severus banned women from appearing in the arena in any role at all!

There were many types of gladiator with different fighting styles, weapons, and armor. Lanistas liked to pair gladiators to make interesting and long fights. Often nimble gladiators with little armor would fight larger gladiators weighed down by heavy armor. Here is an A-Z of gladiator types.

ANDABATAE

The bizarre andabatae were horsemen dressed in heavy chain mail who wore helmets without any eyeholes. They had to slash blindly about using the sounds of the horses to try to find each other!

BUSTUARIUS

In the very early days of gladiatorial fights some men were pushed into the arena without any training at all. Their role was simply to be killed by the more experienced and better trained gladiators. These unfortunate fighters were called bustuarius.

CRUPELLARIUS

These men wore jointed metal armor that covered them from head to toe as well as a metal shield and helmet. They are mentioned only for a short period between about AD 80 and AD 140.

DIMARCHAERUS

Dimarchaerus were armed with two long, curved swords but no shields. The only armor they had consisted of cloth or leather padding around the arms. It seems to have been common to match them against heavily armored opponents such as the hoplomachus.

EQUITES

Equites were usually the first gladiators to appear in the arena. On horseback, wearing a tunic, their lower legs and the right arm were protected by quilted armor. They carried a small round shield. The helmet was a simple round skull cap. The face was usually covered by a hinged visor. The equites fought using a long lance and a short sword.

HOPLOMACHUS

This type of gladiator was based on the heavily armed Greek hoplite soldier. He wore a Greek style helmet and carried a round shield. The hoplomachus wore long metal greaves over quilted padding on their legs. They were armed with a long spear. If the spear broke, the hoplomachus had a short dagger to use as a final weapon.

LAQUERARIUS

A laquerarius was armed with a lasso and a short sword. Their only armor was padding on the arms. They were probably based on warriors from the Caspian Sea area who used lassos in battle.

MURMILLO

Murmillos wore a spectacular helmet. It had a wide brim with a large, metal crest, sometimes decorated with feathers or horsehair. The name murmillo is a Greek word for a type of fish. Some helmets had fish scales carved on them. Murmillos carried a large, rectangular shield and a metal greave on the left leg, over quilted padding. The sword arm was also covered in padding. The armor, sword, and shield were heavy. He often fought more lightly armed Thracian or the hoplomachus gladiators.

PAEGNIARIUS

The paegniarius were a type of clown. They dressed in imitation gladiator armor, often with humorous designs on their shields or their armor. They entertained the crowd while scenery was being changed or gladiators were getting ready. They poked fun at the fighting techniques of the gladiators, or mocked topical events.

PROVOCATOR

Provocators usually fought against other provocators. They carried a shield, short greaves and quilted sword arm armor. They fought using a short sword. Their helmet had no brim or crest. It was made from a single sheet of bronze and reached down to the back of the neck. They wore a small breastplate secured by leather straps. Provocators fought fairly static sword fights. Skill with the shield would have been very important.

RETIARIUS

The retiarius had no shield, helmet, or greaves. His armor was just quilted padding on the left arm and a metal shoulder plate. He fought with a long trident with a stout wooden handle and sharp prongs. He also carried a circular fishing net tied to his left wrist by long strings. He attacked by casting his net in the hope of tangling his opponent, and then stabbing him with the trident. If the net got caught by the other gladiator, the retiarius had a short knife to cut himself free.

A retiarius fights a secutor.

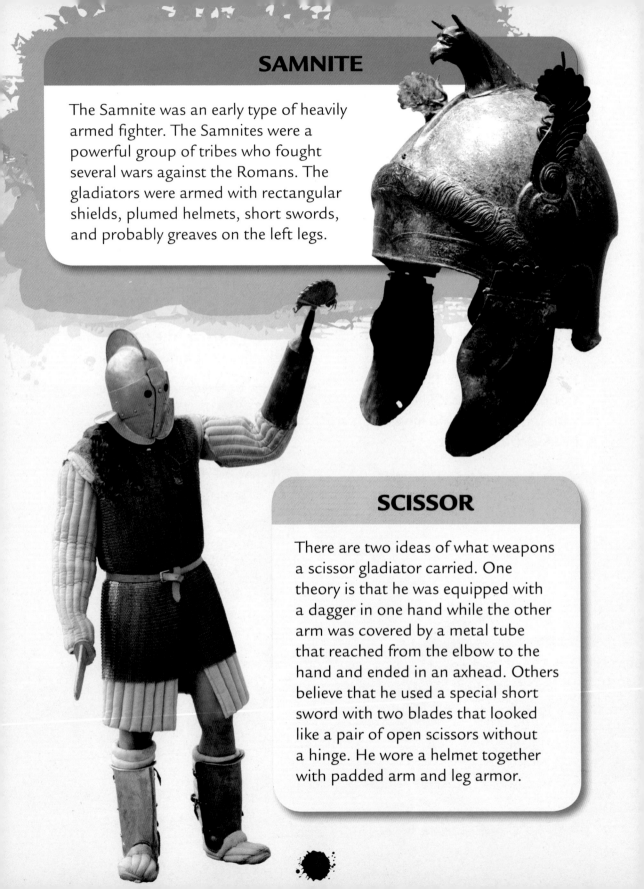

SAMNITE

The Samnite was an early type of heavily armed fighter. The Samnites were a powerful group of tribes who fought several wars against the Romans. The gladiators were armed with rectangular shields, plumed helmets, short swords, and probably greaves on the left legs.

SCISSOR

There are two ideas of what weapons a scissor gladiator carried. One theory is that he was equipped with a dagger in one hand while the other arm was covered by a metal tube that reached from the elbow to the hand and ended in an axhead. Others believe that he used a special short sword with two blades that looked like a pair of open scissors without a hinge. He wore a helmet together with padded arm and leg armor.

SECUTOR

Secutors often fought retiarius. The secutor's helmet was smooth with fish fin decorations. It had a solid metal visor with two small eye holes. The secutor could not see much, but his eyes and face were protected against jabs from the retiarius' trident. Fights between the lightly armed retiarius and the heavily armored secutor were popular with the crowds. The secutor tried to finish a fight quickly. The retiarius either tangled the secutor in his net or waited until the secutor tired under the weight of his armor.

THRAEX

Thraex gladiators were based on soldiers from Thrace, what is now Bulgaria. Their helmets had a curved crest decorated with a griffin, and were sometimes decorated with feathers. Their shields were square. Leg greaves were worn from the ankle to above the knee. The thighs and sword arm were covered in quilted padding. They were armed with a short, curved sword to slash or stab with.

VENATORES

Venatores were not strictly gladiators. They specialized in wild animal hunts. They also performed with animals, doing tricks such as putting their arm in a lion's mouth, leading lions on a leash while riding a camel, and even getting an elephant to walk a tightrope!

A flask showing a murmillo beating a thraex

The Emperors

Although most gladiators were slaves, some were free men who agreed to fight for a variety of reasons. Perhaps the most astonishing fact is that some Roman emperors fought in the arena as gladiators.

CALIGULA

Emperor Caligula was a skilled swordsman. As a young man he had trained as a soldier. While emperor, he trained to be a Thraex gladiator! He appeared in public dressed as a Thraex several times. He took part in sparring contests with blunted weapons against famous gladiators.

COMMODUS

Commodus became Emperor when he was 18 years old. He was very proud of his muscular figure and skills with weapons. He appeared many times in the arena to fight against famous gladiators. The gladiators had all agreed to surrender and ask for mercy after fighting for several minutes! Commodus also fought against lions, elephants, and once killed an ostrich by throwing a dart at its neck.

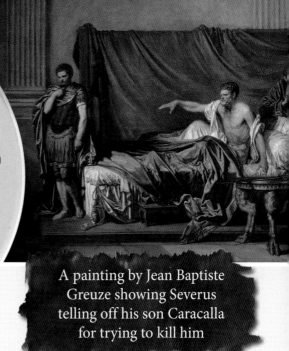

That's Fearless!

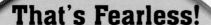

Caracalla and his brother Geta inherited the empire from their father Septimius Severus. After 10 months Caracalla had Geta murdered! Caracalla loved mixing with soldiers and gladiators, and showing off his skills with weapons. He entertained dinner guests by slipping away between courses and returning wearing a gladiator's helmet. After he defeated his opponent he would reveal his face to the applause of his guests.

A painting by Jean Baptiste Greuze showing Severus telling off his son Caracalla for trying to kill him

HADRIAN

Hadrian served in the Roman army for years before becoming Emperor. He spent most of his reign traveling around the Empire. To boost his popularity back in Rome he organized spectacular free entertainment, including gladiatorial combats. Hadrian is said to have fought as a gladiator in displays for his friends and army colleagues.

While in Europe Hadrian oversaw the building of a vast wall, right across northern England.

Animal Hunts

Entertainment involving animals was popular in the gladiator arena. The Romans enjoyed watching bizarre shows, such as chimpanzees driving chariots drawn by camels, or dancing elephants. Most entertainment involved bloodshed of one form or another, however.

The politician Sulla gained favor by organizing a huge animal hunt. He built a hunting ground surrounded by wooden walls and viewing platforms in fields near Rome. When the audience was in place Sulla let loose bears, boars, deer, and wolves to be hunted by teams of armed men with hunting dogs.

General Scipio defeated an army in North Africa. To boost his popularity before an election he put on a show of African animals brought back with him. Crocodiles, gazelles, and an elephant were paraded through the Forum Romanum to the delight of the crowd. He won his election.

That's Fearless!

The wild bulls of ancient Rome are now extinct. Known as **aurochs**, they were twice the size of domestic bulls. In the arena the bullfighters rarely killed the bull. Instead they tried to hook ribbons to its horns, jump over its back, or pole vault over its head. That's dangerous!

An illustration of what an auroch looked like

Romans like to watch animals hunting each other as they would in the wild. The arena would be decorated with bushes and trees, then some gazelles would be let loose. Finally a lion would be put in the arena to hunt the gazelles. Other natural hunts included wolves hunting deer, tigers attacking buffalo, and crocodiles killing deer. Often two hunting animals would be used in the hope that they would turn on each other to fight over the meal!

ANIMAL PAIRINGS

One way the Romans used to get animals to fight was to chain them together. Each animal would resent being tied to the chain and blame the other animal for it. A bull chained to a bear was a favorite, as was a bull chained to a lion. Other pairings could be bizarre. A wolf was once chained to a seal, a bear to a python, and a lion to a crocodile!

Hunts in the Arena

Specialist gladiators called venatores were trained to fight animals, and the more dangerous the animals the better. Most venatores had no armor. They relied on their skill with hunting weapons and their speed to keep themselves alive.

Most animal combats in the arena featured a spinning door. This heavy wooden door was used as a shelter, and as a weapon. A lion hunter would goad the lion until it charged, then run to the door and slam it in the lion's face to knock it unconscious!

During animal fights empty barrels were left scattered around the arena. If a hunter got into trouble he could jump into the barrel. The attacking animal would paw at the wood until it got bored and left. The man could then come out and continue the hunt.

Some animal hunters were given suits of armor to wear, usually mail that covered them from head to foot. They needed their armor as their weapons were only short daggers - not much use when facing a lion or a bear!

Emperor Probus laid on a special animal hunt. An entire German forest, complete with mature trees larger than any seen in Rome, were dragged from a forest to form the backdrop to an amazing animal hunt. 300 bears, hundreds of wolves, aurochs, and other forest animals were hunted.

The demand for animals for the arena became huge. Some species were driven to **extinction**, such as the black-maned Balkan lion, the small North African elephant, and the desert cheetah.

That's Fearless!

One man earned huge sums of money by killing lions with his bare hands. He forced the lion's mouth open, then rammed his fist down the lion's throat and choked it!

CATCHING ANIMALS

An entire industry was set up to capture wild animals for use in the arena. Expeditions of men went to places such as Africa to catch lions, leopards, elephants, giraffes, and gazelles, and bring them back to Rome.

Leopards were caught by digging a deep pit with a low wall around it, just high enough to stop the leopard seeing the pit behind. A goat was put in the pit. Hearing the goat's cries, the hungry leopard would leap over the wall and fall into the pit. The leopard was then put in a cage, hauled up, and put on a cart.

Gladiator Timeline

The term BCE stands for "before the Christian era" and measures time before our modern calendar began. If you see AD before a date that means it is a year in our calendar. Anything that happened before AD 1 will have BCE written after it. Years before AD 1 go backward rather than forward, so 100 BCE is one hundred years after 200 BCE!

264 BCE First Gladiator Games
First gladiator fight in Rome takes place during the funeral of Decimus Junius Brutus arranged by his two sons. Three pairs of slaves fought to the death in the cattle market watched by large crowds.

c.80 BCE Thraex
First appearance of Thracian prisoners of war in the arena. They are later imitated by the Thraex gladiator.

89 BCE Samnites
Samnite prisoners of war appear as gladiators in games organized by general Sulla as part of an election campaign. This starts a fashion for prisoners of war using their native weapons appearing as gladiators.

300 BCE

200 BCE

100 BCE

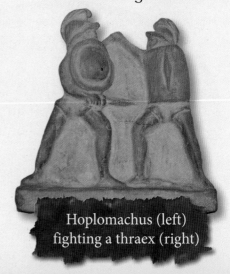

Hoplomachus (left) fighting a thraex (right)

79 BCE Charging Elephants!

General Pompey brings twenty elephants from North Africa to the arena. The show goes wrong when the elephants charge the barriers and nearly break through to attack the crowd! Pompey loses the election and returns to the army.

75 BCE

c.75 BCE Missus

The first known use of the missus. Until this date all combats seem to have been to the death. A defeated gladiator would raise the first finger of his left hand to ask for mercy. If he had fought well he may be allowed to live.

50 BCE

c.70 BCE The Gauls

Gaulish prisoners of war first appear in the arena using long Gaulish swords, large oval shields and protective mail shirts as well as rounded Gaulish helmets.

1 BCE

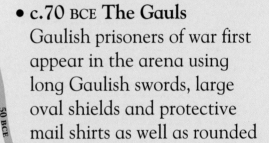

Asking for the missus

46 BCE Caesar's Great Games

Julius Caesar organizes the biggest games so far, with theatre shows, chariot racing, dancers, trick riders, and jugglers. An artificial lake was built for fake naval fights between real war ships! The gladiator arena featured hidden tunnels, trapdoors, and lifts.

AD 52 Hail Caesar!

Gladiators about to fight in front of Emperor Claudius saluted him and shouted "Ave Caesar morituri te salutant," meaning "Hail, Caesar, we who are about to die salute you." This is the only time this famous salute is recorded having taken place.

AD 248 Amazing Games

To celebrate the 1,000th anniversary of the founding of Rome, Emperor Philip the Arab organized an astonishing gladiator games. An artificial lake was built for naval battles. Thousands of animals were killed, and gladiatorial combats were held involving over 4,000 fighters!

AD 1

AD 100

AD 200

AD 80 A Vast Arena is Built

Emperor Titus opened the Colosseum as a venue for gladiator fights and other spectacles. The stadium held 50,000 spectators and has canvas screens to shade the audience from the sun. Under the arena, tunnels led to trapdoors and lifts for spectacular surprises during the show.

AD 82 Big Ludus

The Ludus Magnus "The Big School" is built in Rome by Emperor Domitian to train and supply gladiators, animal hunters, and other performers to the Colosseum in Rome. It is the biggest gladiator school in the Empire!

That's Fearless!

In AD 404 Christian monk Telemachus of Asia leaped into the arena and separated a pair of fighting gladiators! He then preached to the audience about brotherly love. Pagans in the crowd attacked him, while Christians rushed to defend him. Many people were killed, including Telemachus. Emperor Honorius promptly banned gladiatorial combats in Rome!

AD 423 Games Ban Lifted
Emperor Valentinian III lifts the ban on gladiatorial combats in Rome.

AD 300

AD 400

AD 500

AD 366 Gladiator Army
During a hotly contested election for the position of Christian Bishop of Rome, one candidate named Damasus hired a small army of gladiators to attack the supporters of his rival Ursinus! 137 people were killed in the fighting, and Damasus became Pope!

AD 434 Last Games
Last known gladiatorial combat in Rome. The Empire was crumbling in the face of barbarian invasions and no Emperor had the time or money to spend on gladiatorial shows.

AD 536 Last Animal Show
Last known wild animal show in Rome. The show was held by the Byzantine general Belisarius to celebrate having freed Rome from the Goths.

What Do You Know?

Can you answer these questions about the Gladiators?

1. What food did gladiators eat a lot of in the ludus?

2. When did the first gladiator combat take place?

3. When did the last gladiator combat take place?

4. Which type of gladiator fought with a net and trident like a fisherman?

5. How did a gladiator ask for mercy?

6. What type of gladiator used equipment based on Greek soldiers?

7. What was the man who owned and trained gladiators called?

8. Were gladiator fights originally staged at weddings or funerals?

9. Which Christian monk was killed by the crowd when trying to stop a gladiator combat?

10. What was the name of the famous gladiator who led a breakout from a ludus at Capua?

Answers on page 48

Further Information

Books

Barnham, Kay. *Gory Gladiators*. London, UK: Wayland, 2014.

Burgan, Michael. *Life as a Gladiator*. Mankato, MN: Capstone, 2010.

Greathead, Helen. *Gladiator*, London, UK: A&C Black, 2007.

Matthews, Rupert. *100 Facts on Gladiators*. Essex, UK: Bardfield Press, 2007.

Websites

Colosseum website (English version):
http://archeoroma.beniculturali.it/en/archaeological-site/colosseum

Gladiator: Dressed to Kill Game
http://www.bbc.co.uk/history/ancient/romans/launch_gms_gladiator.shtml

Gladiator page on Ancient History website:
http://www.ancient.eu/gladiator/

Publisher's note to educators and parents: Our editors have carefully reviewed these websites to ensure that they are suitable for students. Many websites change frequently, however, and we cannot guarantee that a site's future contents will continue to meet our high standards of quality and educational value. Be advised that students should be closely supervised whenever they access the Internet.

Glossary

amphitheaters A building with seats rising in curved rows around an open space on which games and plays take place.

aurochs An extinct type of wild cattle that lived across Europe in Roman times. An aurochs bull stood 6 foot 6 inches (2 m) tall at the shoulder and weighed around a ton (1,000 kg).

Campania The ancient name for southern Italy. In ancient times the area was populated by Greek-speaking people.

chariot A light, two-wheeled vehicle pulled by horses used in warfare or for racing.

dictator In ancient Rome, a person elected to have absolute power over the army and government for a limited period of time to deal with an emergency.

editor The person organizing and paying for the gladiatorial show.

extinction When a species dies out and no longer exists.

Gaul A person from Gaul, an ancient country that covered roughly the area of modern France, Belgium, and Netherlands.

lanista The name given to the man who owned, trained, and managed gladiators.

ludus The name given to the buildings where gladiators lived and trained.

missus A gladiator who lost a combat but was allowed to leave the arena alive was said to have been granted the missus. The world means "alive."

munus An event held to celebrate the life and works of a recently deceased person. The word literally means "duty."

novicius A man training as a gladiator who is not yet ready to fight in the arena.

noxii Criminals condemned to death for crimes against the state.

oath A promise made in front of a god or gods.

palus A wooden post used in gladiator training.

Pergamon A wealthy ancient Greek city in what is now Turkey, it was one of the largest cities in the world.

sacrificed Killed as an offering made to a god or goddess.

Samnite A person from a nation that lived in eastern Italy in ancient times. They fought several wars against Rome.

Saturnalia An ancient Roman festival held from December 17 to December 23 to honor the creator god Saturn.

slaves People owned by another person. Slaves had to do what they were told or were savagely punished.

Thracian A person from Thrace, an ancient kingdom in approximately the place where Bulgaria is today.

venatores A type of Roman gladiator who specialized in hunting wild animals.

Index

Answers to Quiz

1. porridge
2. 264 BCE
3. AD 434
4. the retiarius
5. by throwing down his weapons
   and pointing upwards with the
   first finger of his left hand
6. the hoplomachus
7. a lanista
8. funerals
9. Telemachus
10. Spartacus